The
Arms, Flags
and Emblems
of Canada

Published by Deneau Publishers in
co-operation with the Department of the
Secretary of State and the
Canadian Government Publishing Centre,
Supply and Services Canada.

©Minister of Supply & Services Canada 1981

Published by Deneau Publishers & Company Ltd. in co-operation with the Department of the Secretary of State and the Canadian Government Publishing Centre, Supply and Services Canada.

First edition, 1978
Second (revised) edition, 1981
Catalogue No. S2-21/1981E
ISBN 0-88879-030-9

PAUL GILBERT DESIGN LIMITED

Table of contents

Acknowledgement
The Department of the Secretary of State acknowledges the contribution of Auguste Vachon, Chief of the Medal, Heraldry and Costume Section, Public Archives of Canada, who wrote the Introduction, compiled and translated the Glossary, and translated the blazons.

Introduction

Symbols have the remarkable capacity of expressing varied and frequently complex ideas through imagery. The symbolism of the coats of arms, flags and emblems discussed here reflects the history, beliefs, ideologies and aspirations of communities living in a specific territory with particular geographical characteristics, flora and fauna. Heraldry, which is based on sound and precise laws, unites and expresses in images the most essential elements of this collective consciousness.

Heraldry is a product of the Middle Ages. In those days knights wore visored helmets in battle and in order to be recognized they carried distinctive signs such as brilliantly coloured figures painted on their shields and banners which they adopted as their own. The holding of tournaments, one of the principal functions of the heralds of arms, played an important part in developing the rules and terminology of heraldry and in making it a flourishing art.

The arms chosen by Canada's provinces and territories are not, except for those of Ontario, stylized. Thus their designs may vary from artist to artist although their elements cannot be altered. The Ontario arms are stylized and the artistic design must remain unchanged.

The provinces and territories chose and approved the design of their flags.

The provinces are presented in the order of their entry into Confederation. The territories follow the provinces in alphabetical order.

A full achievement of arms includes the shield and all its accessories, several of which correspond to different components of a knight's armour:

Arms — Consists of the devices displayed on the shield and corresponds to the symbols depicted on the defensive shields of mediaeval knights.

Helmet — Is placed above the shield and corresponds to the helmet worn by knights to protect their heads from blows.

Lambrequin or mantling — A piece of cloth which the knight placed over his helmet for protection from the heat of the sun. They are portrayed with many curly frills as if they had been cut and torn during a battle or tournament. The present practice is for the lambrequins to be of the main colour of the shield and their lining of the principal metal.

Torse or crest wreath — Wreath formed of the two twisted silk ribbons used to secure the lambrequin. One of the ribbons is of the principal metal of the shield, the other of the principal colour.

Crest — Helmet ornament. It is the topmost device in an achievement of arms and takes its origin from the practice of attaching small animal figures or other objects to the top of the knight's helmet.

Supporters — Figures on each side of the shield, seemingly supporting or protecting it. Although their origin is not known for certain, some heraldists believe that they were first used to fill the empty spaces left when a shield of arms was engraved on a seal.

Motto — Certain mottos were at one time battle cries, but most seem to have been derived from another source, since they usually express some noble or pious sentiment.

Contrary to general belief, heraldry is a simple and enjoyable science. You need only master a few basic rules and about a hundred heraldic terms to be at ease with it.

Today heraldry is enjoying renewed popularity. This new trend is doubtless partially explained by the need felt by twentieth century man to cling to certain traditional values in the face of the changing conditions of life.

Canada

Arms

Granted by proclamation of King George V, dated 21st November 1921.

Arms
Tierced in Fesse: the first and second divisions containing the quarterly coat following, namely, 1st Gules, three Lions passant guardant in pale Or, 2nd, Or, a Lion rampant within a double Tressure Fleury-counter-Fleury Gules, 3rd, Azure, a Harp Or stringed Argent, 4th, Azure, three Fleurs-de-Lis, Or, and the third division Argent, three Maple leaves conjoined on one Stem proper.

Helmet
A Royal helmet.

Mantling
Argent doubled gules.

Crest
On a Wreath of the Colours Argent and Gules a Lion passant guardant Or imperially crowned proper and holding in the dexter Paw a Maple leaf Gules.

Supporters
On the dexter a Lion rampant Or holding a Lance Argent, Point Or, flying therefrom to the dexter the Union Flag, and on the sinister, a Unicorn Argent armed crined and unguled Or, gorged with a Coronet composed of Crosses patée and Fleurs-de-Lis a Chain affixed thereto reflexed of the last, and holding a like Lance flying therefrom to the sinister a Banner Azure charged with three Fleurs-de-Lis Or.

Crown
The whole ensigned with the Imperial Crown proper.

Motto
Upon a Wreath composed of Roses, Thistles, Shamrocks and Lilies a Scroll Azure inscribed with the motto A MARI USQUE AD MARE

In May 1868, a Royal Warrant of Queen Victoria granted armorial bearings to the first four provinces which had joined Confederation the year before: Ontario, Québec, Nova Scotia and New Brunswick. The Warrant stated that the "Arms of the said Four Provinces Quarterly" would be used to design a Great Seal for Canada. For some reason, the quartered arms were not used when a Great Seal was designed shortly after, but they were soon adopted through usage as the arms of the Dominion. As other provinces joined the Confederation, their arms were incorporated into this federal composite design. Because the result became crowded and confusing, as well as being heraldically unsatisfactory, the Canadian Government submitted a request to the Sovereign for a proper grant of arms. The request was approved and the Arms assigned to Canada were appointed and declared in the proclamation of His Majesty King George V dated November 21, 1921, on the basis of Canadian Order in Council P.C. 1496 dated April 30, 1921. In 1957 the Canadian Government approved the adoption of an amended version of the Arms which corrected certain of the colours, simplified the design for reproduction purposes and, in accordance with the expressed wishes of the Queen, adopted the St. Edward's Crown in place of the Tudor Crown which had been in use since Edward VII.

Significance and use of the Arms of Canada

The Arms of Canada, containing the Arms of England, Scotland, Ireland and royalist France and the emblem of Canada, symbolize Canada's national sovereignty and give recognition to the contribution of these countries to the settlement and early development of Canada.

The arms are used by Canada on federal government possessions such as proclamations, passports and other official documents as well as rank badges of some members of the Canadian Armed Forces. The Trade Marks Act (ch. T-10, RSC 1970) protects the Arms of Canada against unauthorized use.

8 Canada

National Flag

The National Flag, adopted by Parliament on October 22, 1964, was proclaimed by Her Majesty Queen Elizabeth II on February 15, 1965. It is a red flag of the proportions two by length and one by width, containing in its centre a white square the width of the flag with a single red maple leaf centred therein. The eleven-point maple leaf in the flag design is stylized or conventional in form, as is common when things found in nature are incorporated into flags, banners or arms. Red and white are the official colours for Canada, declared and appointed by King George V on November 21, 1921 in a proclamation of Canada's Coat of Arms recommended to His Majesty by the Canadian Government.

Emblems of Canada

Maple Leaf

The history of the maple leaf as a Canadian emblem is almost as long as that of the beaver. It is said that the maple leaf was looked upon as a fit emblem for Canadians as early as 1700 if not before. When the Prince of Wales visited Canada in 1860, members of the welcoming procession wore the maple leaf as "the emblem of the land of their birth." In 1867 Alexander Muir, schoolmaster and poet, composed "The Maple Leaf Forever" as Canada's Confederation song. The following year, Queen Victoria granted coats of arms bearing maple leaves to the provinces of Ontario and Québec. In 1921 a similar sprig of maple leaves was used as the distinctively Canadian symbol in the new Coat of Arms for Canada granted by King George V. For many years the maple leaf has also been used as a symbol and mark of identity by the Canadian Armed Forces. During World War I it was the dominant symbol of the regimental badges of almost all battalions of the Canadian Expeditionary Force. In World War II, Canadians again used the maple leaf to represent their nationality, wearing it on regimental badges and using it to designate everything Canadian from roadways to ships. The maple leaf was confirmed as an official national symbol in 1965 with the proclamation on February 15th of the national flag of Canada.

Beaver

The Huron Indians used the beaver as an emblem of their tribe. Such distinctive tribal emblems were affixed by Indians to treaties they signed with early settlers.

The beaver probably first appeared as a heraldic symbol of Canada as the crest of the coat of arms granted in 1633 to Sir William Alexander by King Charles I. In 1673 Count Frontenac, governor general of New France, proposed for the City of Québec armorial bearings containing "a Beaver Sable on a Chief Or" and, as early as 1678, the Hudson's Bay Company placed four beavers on its adopted arms. The beaver was also included in the coat of arms adopted by Montréal in 1833 following its incorporation as a city.

The beaver was so important and valuable to the fur trade that its pelt became a standard article of barter and trade. It was used as a basis for currency when the Hudson's Bay Company issued coin equal in value to a beaver pelt. By the 19th century the beaver had gained considerable acceptance and recognition as a Canadian symbol, appearing on the mast-head of *Le Canadien,* a newspaper published in Lower Canada; as an emblem of the St-Jean-Baptiste Society; and on the crest of the Canadian Pacific Railway. When Canada issued its first postage stamp on April 23, 1851, the beaver was the main feature of its design and thereafter the stamp was known as the "Three Penny Beaver."

The beaver finally attained official status as an emblem of Canada in 1975 when an "Act to provide for the recognition of the beaver *(Castor canadensis)* as a symbol of the sovereignty of Canada" received Royal Assent on March 24, 1975.

Ontario

VT INCEPIT   SIC PERMANET

FIDELIS

Arms

Granted by Royal Warrant of Queen Victoria, dated 26th May 1868. Crest, supporters and motto granted by Royal Warrant of King Edward VII, dated 27th February 1909.

Arms
Vert, a Sprig of three leaves of Maple slipped Or, on a Chief Argent, the Cross of St. George.

Crest
Upon a Wreath of the Colours a Bear passant Sable.

Supporters
On the dexter side, a Moose, and on the sinister side a Canadian Deer both proper.

Motto
UT INCEPIT FIDELIS SIC PERMANET
(Loyal she began and loyal she remains.)

16   Ontario

Flag

Given Royal Assent on April 14, 1965 and proclaimed into force on May 21, 1965, the flag of Ontario is the Red Ensign of the proportions two by length and one by width with the Royal Union Flag (commonly known as Union Jack) occupying the upper quarter nearest the staff and the Shield of the Arms of the province placed on the fly.

Flown on Ships and Boats

14. The Canadian Flag is the proper national colours for all Canadian ships and boats including pleasure craft. The Canada Shipping Act provides that a Canadian ship shall hoist the Flag on a signal being made to her by one of Her Majesty's ships, or any ship in the service of and belonging to the Government of Canada; on entering or leaving any foreign port; and if of 50 tons gross tonnage or upwards, on entering or leaving any Commonwealth port.

15. Foreign vessels may wear the Canadian Flag as a "courtesy flag" when in a Canadian port. The Flag is customarily flown from the foremast.

16. The following rules govern merchant vessels and pleasure craft as a matter of custom:
(a) The Flag should be worn in harbour and in territorial waters but need not be worn while under way on the high seas unless the vessel wishes to identify her nationality to another ship.
(b) Wherever possible, the proper place for a vessel to display the national colours is at the stern, except that when at sea, the Flag may be flown from a gaff.
(c) When in harbour the Flag should be hoisted at 0800 hours and lowered at sunset.
(d) When a merchant ship passes, or is passed by a navy vessel of any nationality, the merchant ship should dip the Flag as a courtesy. If on a staff, the lowest corner of the Flag should be brought to the level of the rail and kept there until the salutation is acknowledged by the naval vessel; if flown from a gaff, the Flag should be lowered to six feet above the level of the deck, until the salute is acknowledged.
(e) In times of mourning the Flag may be flown at half-mast, which places the upper corner of the Flag next to the staff at approximately three-quarters of full-hoist. As on land, a flag hoisted to, or lowered from, half-mast position must first be hauled close-up.

17. The Union Flag will, where physical arrangements make it possible, be flown along with the Canadian Flag at federal buildings, airports, and military bases and establishments within Canada on the date of the official observance of the Queen's birthday, the Anniversary of the Statute of Westminster (December 11th), and on the occasions of Royal Visits

When more than three flags are flown together.

and certain Commonwealth gatherings in Canada.

18. The Union Flag may be flown with the Canadian Flag at the National War Memorial (1914-1918) and at similarly appropriate federal locations in Canada, in connection with ceremonies marking anniversaries of events in which Canadian forces participated with other Commonwealth forces.

19. It is a matter of judgment for individuals and organizations in Canada to fly the Union Flag as seems appropriate to them, having regard to the form of approval given by Parliament to that Flag.

20. The United Nations Flag is flown with the Canadian Flag on Parliament Hill, Ottawa, on United Nations Day, October 24th, and by special arrangement on other occasions including visits to the Capital by the Secretary-General or his representative.

21. When the Queen is in Canada, Her Majesty's Personal Canadian Flag is flown, day and night, at any building in which she is in residence or in which she is attending a state or public function. Generally the Flag is also flown behind the saluting base when she conducts troop inspections and on Her Majesty's ships when the Queen is aboard.

22. Similar provision is made for the use of the Governor General's Flag when His Excellency is present.

23. These Flags, like all personal flags or standards, may not be used by others, and they are never half-masted.

Design of the Canadian Flag

1. Technical description

A red flag of the proportions two by length and one by width (or 64 units in length and 32 units in width (depth) as shown in the accompanying diagram), containing in its centre a white square the width of the flag, with a single red maple leaf centred therein.

2. Colours

The colours red and white in the Canadian Flag are the same as those that were used in the Canadian Red Ensign and are found in the Union Jack.

3. Heraldic Description

Gules (red) on a Canadian pale argent (white) a maple leaf of the first.

Flagpoles and Flags

What follows is illustrative of standards used for flags flown at federal government buildings:

Length of Flag Pole	Size of Flag
17 to 20 ft./ 5.5 to 6.5 m	3 x 6 ft./1 x 2 m
30 to 35 ft./ 9.75 to 11.5 m	4½ x 9 ft./1.5 x 3 m
40 to 45 ft./ 13 to 14.75 m	6 x 12 ft./2 x 4 m
50 ft./16.25 m	7½ x 15 ft./2.5 x 5 m

Floral Emblem

White Trillium (*Trillium grandiflorum*). Adopted in 1937.

Popularly known as the White Trillium or wake-robin, the flower was recommended as the floral emblem of Ontario by the Ontario Horticultural Society. The White Trillium blooms in great abundance in Ontario's deciduous forests during late April and May. It cannot be picked without taking all the foliage which is needed to develop the bulbous root for the following season's bloom.

Québec

JE ME SOUVIENS

Arms

Approved and authorized by Provincial Order in Council of 9th December 1939.

Arms
Tierced in Fesse: Azure, three Fleurs-de-Lis Or; Gules, a Lion passant guardant Or armed and langued Azure; Or, a Sugar Maple Sprig with three Leaves Vert veined Or.

Crest
The Royal Crown.

Motto
Below the shield a scroll Argent, surrounded by a bordure Azure inscribed with the motto "JE ME SOUVIENS" Azure.

The arms symbolize the joining of the traditions of royalist France and of Britain in the new land of Canada. Below the shield is a scroll, with a motto meaning "I remember," added in 1883 by Mr. Eugène Taché, architect of the Parliament building.

Flag

The flag, generally designated by the name of the fleurdelisé flag, bears a white cross on a sky-blue background with a white fleur-de-lis positioned in the centre of each of the quarters formed by the cross. The proportions of the flag are six units wide by four units deep with the cross being one unit in both middle directions. The fleurdelisé flag was adopted as the official flag of the Province of Québec on January 21, 1948 by an order of the Lieutenant-Governor in Council and by an act assented to on March 9, 1950.

Floral Emblem

Madonna Lily (*Lilium candidum*). Adopted in 1963.
This easily cultivated, pure white lily is generally known
as the Madonna Lily although it has also been called the
Annunciation Lily, the Lent Lily, the Bourbon Lily and
the St. Joseph's Lily. It was adopted as the official floral
emblem of Québec on March 13, 1963.

Nova Scotia

Arms

First granted by Royal Warrant of King Charles I in 1625. Reinstated by Royal Warrant of King George V dated January 19, 1929 to supersede Armorial Ensigns granted May 26, 1868.

Arms

Argent, a Cross of St. Andrew Azure charged with an escutcheon of the Royal Arms of Scotland.

Crest

On a Wreath of the Colours, a branch of Laurel and a Thistle issuing from two Hands conjoined, the one being armed and the other naked, all proper.

Supporters

On the dexter side, an Unicorn Argent armed, crined and unguled Or, and crowned with the Imperial Crown proper, and gorged with a Coronet composed of Crosses patée and Fleurs-de-Lis a Chain affixed thereto passing through the forelegs and reflexed over the back, Or. And on the sinister side, a Savage holding in the exterior Hand an Arrow, proper.

Motto

MUNIT HAEC ET ALTERA VINCIT.

In 1621, King James VI of Scotland and I of England granted to Sir William Alexander all the land between New England and Newfoundland for the formation of a colony which was given the name of New Scotland, or in its Latin form, Nova Scotia. In 1625, James' successor, King Charles I, granted the colony a coat of arms based upon the National Arms of Scotland.

The scroll above the armorial bearings is inscribed with a motto meaning "One defends and the other conquers." The motto is placed on a scroll above the achievement of arms as is done for many Scottish Grants of Arms.

28 Nova Scotia

Flag

The flag of Nova Scotia traces its origin to the Charter of New Scotland granted in 1621 to Sir William Alexander by King James VI of Scotland and I of England. The use of the Arms granted in 1625, without the supporters and crest, as the official flag of the province was granted by Royal Warrant dated January 19, 1929. The Warrant stated that the granted armorial bearings were "to be borne for the said Province of Nova Scotia upon Seals, Shields, Banners, Flags or otherwise according to the Law of Arms." The proportions of the flag are that its depth is to be three-quarters of its length.

Floral Emblem

Mayflower (*Epigaea repens*). Adopted in 1901.

The trailing arbutus or ground laurel, commonly known as the Mayflower, is a creeping evergreen plant which grows in shaded sandy or rocky soil from Newfoundland to Saskatchewan. It derives its name from the Pilgrims who saw it as the first flower of spring and named it after the ship that brought them to Plymouth Rock.

New Brunswick

·SPEM · REDUXIT·

Arms

Granted by Royal Warrant of Queen Victoria, dated 26th May 1868. Crest and Motto added by Order in Council in 1966.

Arms
Or, on Waves, a Lymphad or ancient Galley with Oars in action, proper on a Chief Gules, a Lion passant guardant Or.

Crest
The Royal Crown.

Motto
SPEM REDUXIT.

The chief is symbolic of the House of Brunswick which was ruling England at the time the province was established and from which the province took its name. Below the chief, the ancient galley symbolizes the province's early shipbuilding industry. This version of the province's Arms was adopted in 1966, at which time the crest of a royal crown was added above the shield and the scroll inscribed with the motto "SPEM REDUXIT" was incorporated below the shield. The motto, meaning "Hope was restored," is taken from the original Great Seal of the province which was used until Confederation. It refers to the new hope of the Loyalists who came to the province after the American War of Independence.

34 New Brunswick

Flag

The design of the official flag of the Province of New Brunswick is taken from the Arms assigned to the province by the Royal Warrant of 1868. The Royal Warrant granting the Arms stated that they could "be borne on Seals, Shields, Banners, Flags or otherwise according to the Law of Arms." The flag was adopted by proclamation on February 24, 1965. It is in a rectangular shape of the proportions four by length and two and one half by width, with the chief occupying the upper one-third part and the remainder of the Arms occupying the lower two-thirds part.

Floral Emblem

Purple Violet (*Viola cucullata*). Adopted in 1936.

Of the many flowers that bloom in the New Brunswick forests in spring, the Purple Violet is probably the one most frequently seen. It was adopted as the province's floral emblem by Order in Council on December 1, 1936 at the request of the New Brunswick Women's Institute.

Manitoba

Arms

Granted by Royal Warrant of King Edward VII, dated 10th May 1905.

Arms

Vert, on a Rock a Buffalo statant proper, on a Chief Argent, the Cross of St. George.

On August 2, 1870, soon after Manitoba joined Confederation, a Great Seal which included the present Coat of Arms was approved by the federal government. In May, 1905 by Royal Warrant, the College of Arms in England registered this design as the province's Arms.

Flag

Given Royal Assent on May 11, 1965 and proclaimed into force on May 12, 1966, the flag of Manitoba is the Red Ensign of the proportions two by length and one by width with the Royal Union Flag (commonly known as Union Jack) occupying the upper quarter nearest the staff and with the shield of the Arms of the province placed on the fly.

Floral Emblem

Prairie Crocus (*Anemone patens*). Adopted in 1906.

This early spring flower, which often is seen pushing through the snow, is known in Manitoba as the Prairie Crocus. The flower was chosen by the children of Manitoba through an informal vote conducted in the province's schools and was officially adopted on March 16, 1906.

British Columbia

Arms

Granted by Royal Warrant of King Edward VII, dated 31st March 1906. Crest and supporters have become part of the provincial achievement through usage.

Arms
Argent three Bars wavy Azure, issuant from the base a demi-Sun in splendour proper, on a Chief the Union Device charged in the centre point with an antique Crown Or.

Crest
Upon an Imperial Crown proper, a Lion statant guardant Imperially crowned, all Or.

Supporters
On the dexter side, a Wapiti Stag, proper. On the sinister side, a Ram of the OVIS MONTANA, proper.

Motto
SPLENDOR SINE OCCASU.

The chief at the top of the shield is a Royal Union Flag (commonly known as Union Jack) with an antique gold crown in its centre, symbolizing the province's origin as a British colony. Below the chief, on a ground of blue and silver wavy bars representing the Pacific Ocean, a gold half-sun signifies British Columbia's location as the most westerly province of Canada. Below the shield a scroll is inscribed with a motto meaning "Splendor without diminishment."

46 British Columbia

Flag

The flag takes its design from the shield, without crest
or supporters, as granted by Royal Warrant dated March
31, 1906. The Royal Warrant stated that the Granted
Arms could "be borne for the said Province on Seals,
Shields, Banners, Flags, or otherwise according to the
Law of Arms." The display of British Columbia's Arms
as the official flag of the province was authorized by
Order in Council dated June 20, 1960. The flag is
of the proportion five units wide by three units deep.

48   British Columbia

Floral Emblem

Pacific Dogwood (*Cornus nuttallii*). Adopted in 1956. The Pacific Dogwood is the largest of its species and reaches its greatest size in the forests of southwestern British Columbia and the Puget Sound district of the United States. Growing from 20 to 40 feet high, the tree produces showy white blossoms in the early spring and red berries and brilliant foliage in the autumn.

Prince Edward Island

Arms

Granted by Royal Warrant of King Edward VII, dated 30th May 1905.

Arms

Argent on an Island Vert, to the sinister an Oak Tree fructed, to the dexter thereof three Oak saplings sprouting all proper, on a Chief Gules a Lion passant guardant Or.

Motto

PARVA SUB INGENTI.

The Arms of Prince Edward Island have their origin in the official Seal which was assigned to the Island by King George III under an Order in Council dated July 14, 1769. The configuration described therein came into use as the arms of the province and was properly assigned as such by Royal Warrant. Tradition suggests that the mature tree is the Oak of England and the three saplings represent the province's three counties named King's, Queen's and Prince. The scroll below the shield is inscribed with a motto meaning "The small under the protection of the great."

52 Prince Edward Island

Flag

The flag of Prince Edward Island is that part of the province's arms which is contained within the shield but is of a rectangular shape and is bordered on the three sides away from the mast by alternate bands of red and white. The flag's proportions are six feet in the fly (length), four feet in the hoist (depth) and including the border of alternate rectangles each of which measure ten inches in length and three inches in depth. The flag was officially adopted by Prince Edward Island on March 24, 1964, but the Royal Warrant granting armorial bearings to the province stated that these armorial bearings could be "borne for the said Province on Seals, Shields, Banners, Flags or otherwise according to the Law of Arms."

54 Prince Edward Island

Floral Emblem

Lady's Slipper (*Cypripedium acaule*). Adopted in 1965.

The Lady's Slipper blooms in late May and June and is found in swamps and in forests beneath beechwood, spruce and pine trees. It was first designated as Prince Edward Island's floral emblem by the Legislative Assembly in 1947. A more precise botanical name was stipulated in an amendment to the Floral Emblem Act on March 26, 1965.

Saskatchewan

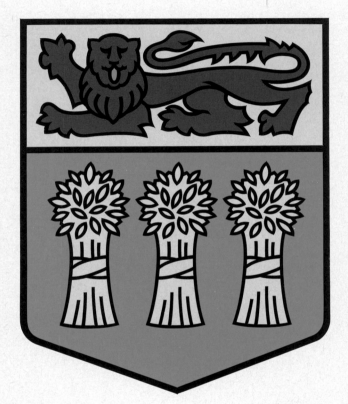

Arms

Granted by Royal Warrant of King Edward VII, dated 25th August 1906.

Arms

Vert, three Garbs in fesse Or, on a Chief of the last, a Lion passant guardant Gules.

58   Saskatchewan

Flag

Saskatchewan's flag was officially dedicated on September 22, 1969. The basic design was adopted from a design submitted by Anthony Drake of Hodgeville in a province-wide competition to establish an official flag for the province. The flag is divided horizontally into two equal parts, the upper segment being green to represent the province's forests, and the lower one being gold to represent the prairie wheat fields. The Arms of Saskatchewan are placed in the first quarter of the flag nearest the staff and the provincial floral emblem is positioned on the fly.

Floral Emblem

Western Red Lily (*Lilium philadelphicum andinum*). Adopted in 1941.

Known also as Prairie Lily, the Western Red Lily blooms in moist meadows and semi wooded areas in Ontario, the Prairies and British Columbia. The Western Red Lily was the official emblem of the Assiniboia Regiment, recruited from one of the oldest settlements in the province.

Alberta

Arms

Granted by Royal Warrant of King Edward VII, dated
30th May 1907. The crest and supporters were
granted by Royal Warrant in 1980, the 75th anniversary of
the founding of the Province of Alberta.

Arms

Azure, in front of a Range of Snow Mountains proper,
a Range of Hills Vert, in base a Wheatfield surmounted by a
Prairie both also proper, on a Chief Argent a St.
George's Cross.

Crest

Upon a Helm with Wreath Argent and Gules a Beaver
couchant upholding on its back the Royal Crown
both proper.

Supporters

On the dexter side a Lion Or armed and langued
Gules and on the sinister side a Pronghorn Antelope
(Antilocapra americana) proper; the Compartment
comprising a grassy mount with the Floral Emblem of the
Province of Alberta, the Wild Rose *(Rosa acicularis)*
growing therefrom proper.

Motto

FORTIS ET LIBER
(Strong and Free)

64   Alberta

Flag

In 1968 the Government of Alberta authorized the design and use of an official flag bearing the Arms of Alberta on a royal ultramarine blue background. The flag was given Royal assent on May 1 and was proclaimed into force on June 1, 1968. The proportions of the flag are two by length and one by width with the provincial Arms seven-elevenths of the width of the flag and displayed in its centre.

Floral Emblem

Wild Rose (*Rosa acicularis*). Adopted in 1930.

The Wild Rose, also known as the Prickly Rose, grows profusely in all parts of the province. Its scarlet berries are a source of winter food for many birds. The flower was chosen as the province's floral emblem by the school children of Alberta.

Newfoundland

Arms

Granted by Royal Letters Patent of King Charles I, dated 1st January 1637.

Arms

Gules a Cross Argent, in the first and fourth quarters a Lion passant guardant crowned Or; in the second and third quarters an Unicorn passant of the second, armed, maned and unguled of the third, and gorged with a Crown, thereto a Chain affixed passing between the forelegs and reflected over his back, of the last.

Mantling

Gules doubled Argent.

Crest

On a Wreath Or and Gules an Elk passant proper.

Supporters

Two Savages of the clime armed and apparelled according to their guise when they go to war.

Motto

QUAERITE PRIME REGNUM DEI (Seek ye First the Kingdom of God).

Flag

The flag of the Province of Newfoundland was assented to on 28th May 1980. It is a white flag of the proportions two by length and one by width bearing four blue triangles on that half of the flag next to the staff, with two triangles bordered in red on that half of the flag in the fly and bearing a golden arrow bordered in red extending from the middle and pointing to the fly of the flag.

72 Newfoundland

Floral Emblem

Pitcher Plant (*Sarracenia purpurea*). Adopted in 1954. The provincial flower of Newfoundland is found in bogs and marshes, blooming in May and June. The flower derives its popular name from its tubular leaves which fold lengthwise to form a deep vase at their base where pools of rain-water collect. More than 100 years ago, Queen Victoria chose the Pitcher Plant to be engraved on the newly minted Newfoundland penny. On June 22, 1954, the Newfoundland Cabinet designated the unusual plant as the official flower of the province.

Northwest Territories

Arms

Authorized and approved by H.M. Queen Elizabeth II, on 24th February 1956.

Arms

Per bend wavy Gules and Vert Billety Or, in sinister chief the Mask of an arctic Fox Argent, on a Chief indented also Argent a Barrulet wavy Azure.

Crest

On a Wreath Argent and Gules a compass Rose proper between two Narwhals haurient and addorsed Or.

The white chief crossed by a wavy blue band in the upper portion of the shield represents the Northwest Passage through the polar ice pack. The lower portion of the shield is divided diagonally by a wavy line which symbolizes the tree line. The green segment of the shield represents the forested areas south of the tree line and the red segment represents the barren lands north of the tree line. The important bases of northern wealth, namely minerals and fur, are symbolized by the gold billets in the green segment and the head of a white fox in the red segment. Surmounting the shield is a crest showing two gold narwhals upon a wreath of red and white, guarding a compass rose which symbolizes the magnetic north pole.

Flag

In 1968 a nation-wide competition was held to obtain a design for a Territorial flag. The design that was chosen was submitted by Robert Bessant of Margaret, Manitoba and adopted as the official flag by the Council of the Northwest Territories on January 1, 1969. The blue panels on either side of the flag represent the lakes and waters of the Northwest Territories. The white centre panel, representing the ice and snow of the north, is equal in width to the two blue panels combined and bears the shield of the Territorial Arms in its centre.

Floral Emblem

Mountain Avens (*Dryas integrifolia*). Adopted in 1957.
The Mountain Avens typically has narrow basal
leaves and supports a single white and yellow flower
on a short stem. This member of the rose family grows
abundantly in the central and eastern Arctic regions of
Canada as well as in parts of the Mackenzie District.

Yukon Territory

Arms

Authorized and approved by H. M. Queen Elizabeth II on 24th February 1956.

Arms

Azure on a Pallet wavy Argent a like Pallet of the field issuant from base two Piles reversed Gules edged also Argent each charged with two Bezants in pale, on a Chief Argent a Cross Gules surmounted of a Roundel Vair.

Crest

On a Wreath Or and Gules a Husky Dog standing on a Mount of Snow proper.

In the centre of the cross a roundel vair in blue and white, symbolizes the fur trade. Below the chief a wavy white and blue vertical stripe represents the Yukon River and refers also to the rivers and creeks where the discovery of placer gold led to the Klondike Gold Rush. The two red spire-like forms against a blue background represent the Yukon's mountains and the two gold discs in each spire symbolize the Territory's mineral resources.

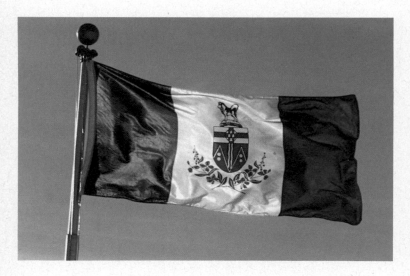

Flag

The Yukon flag was designed by a Haines Junction student, Lynn Lambert, and adopted by the Territorial Council in 1967. It is divided into three equal parts. The third nearest the staff is green, symbolizing the Yukon forests. The middle portion of the flag is white, for snow, with the Arms and floral emblem of the Yukon displayed in its centre. The third furthest from the staff is blue, representing the waters of the Yukon.

Floral Emblem

Fireweed *(Epilobium angustifolium).* Adopted in 1957.
The Fireweed grows in abundance throughout the Yukon Territory. The pale purple flower blooms throughout June, July and August. Hardy as well as beautiful, it is usually the first flower to appear in burned-over areas and thus derives its name.

Historical Flags of Canada

St. George's Cross

It is probable that the first flag to fly over what is now Canadian soil was the English flag of the 15th century, the St. George's Cross. It was carried by John Cabot, a Venetian sailing under English colours, who reached Newfoundland in the last years of the 15th century.

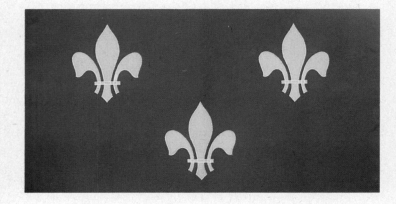

Fleur-de-lis

It is said that the fleur-de-lis first appeared in France in 840 A.D. on a royal sceptre. From the 12th century until the Revolution it was the official emblem of France. When Jacques Cartier landed for the first time at Gaspé in 1534, he planted a cross bearing the Royal Arms of France, a blue shield with three golden fleurs-de-lis. The fleur-de-lis continued as a symbol of French sovereignty in Canada until the Treaty of Paris in 1763 by which the French colonies were ceded to the British Crown. It reappeared as a symbol of French heritage in the first arms granted to the Province of Québec by Queen Victoria in 1868. In 1948 the fleur-de-lis took on a new life in Canada when the Québec government adopted as its provincial flag the fleurdelisé, a flag with a white cross on a sky blue background and a white fleur-de-lis in each of the four sections formed by the cross.

Union Flag

The Royal Union Flag, commonly known as Union Jack, was proclaimed as a royal flag in 1606 after James VI of Scotland became James I of England. It joined together England's flag of a red St. George's Cross on a white background and Scotland's flag of a white St. Andrew's Cross on a dark blue background. In 1708, following their legislative union, England and Scotland adopted the Union Flag as the flag of the United Kingdom. In 1801, after Ireland was taken into the union of Great Britain, the diagonal Cross of St. Patrick, red on white, was incorporated into the flag giving the Union Flag its present configuration.

The original Union Flag first came into use in Canada with the British settlement in Nova Scotia after 1621. In 1869 the Union Flag was incorporated into an official flag for the Lieutenant-Governors of the provinces of Ontario, Québec, Nova Scotia and New Brunswick. The Memorial of the Lords Commissioners of the Admiralty submitted to the Secretary of State for the Colonies a design comprising the Union Jack with the arms of the provinces positioned in its centre.

Although the Red Ensign was widely used in Canada from the time of Confederation, the Union Flag was the affirmed national symbol from 1904 and was the flag under which Canadian troops fought during World War I. On December 18, 1964, Parliament approved the continued use of the Union Flag as a symbol of Canada's membership in the Commonwealth of Nations and of her allegiance to the Crown.

Red Ensign

The Red Ensign was created in 1707 as the flag of the
British merchant marine. The British ensign is red
and bears the Union Flag in the first quarter. Its use in
Canada was first authorized in 1892 by a British Admiralty
warrant providing that the flag, with Canada's shield
in the fly, could be worn on Canadian merchant
ships. In 1924 a Canadian Order in Council provided
that the Canadian Red Ensign could be displayed as the
flag for Canadian federal buildings abroad. Another
Order in Council in 1945 authorized its use on Canadian
federal buildings both within and outside Canada
until Parliament took action for the formal adoption of
a national flag.

Personal Standards

Queen's Personal Canadian Flag

The Queen has adopted a Personal Flag specifically for use in Canada. The design comprises the Arms of Canada charged in the centre with Her Majesty's own device in gold on a blue background, namely the initial "E" surmounted by the St. Edward's Crown within a chaplet of roses. When the Queen is in Canada, Her Majesty's Personal Canadian Flag is flown, day and night, at any building in which she is in residence or in which she is attending a state or public function. Generally the flag is also flown behind the saluting base when she conducts troop inspections and on Her Majesty's ships when the Queen is aboard.

96 Personal Standards

Governor General's Flag

The Crest of the Royal Arms of Canada on a blue field in the proportions of two by height and three by width.

Crest

On a Wreath of the Colours Argent and Gules a Lion passant guardant Or imperially crowned proper and holding in the dexter Paw a Maple leaf Gules.

General Rules for Flying and displaying Flags

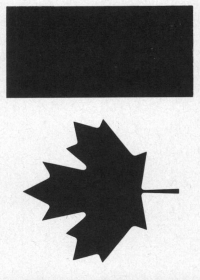

The Flag hung vertically on a wall.

The Canadian Flag was approved by Parliament and on February 15, 1965 proclaimed by Her Majesty The Queen. It is described as a red flag of the proportions two by length and one by width, containing in its centre a white square the width of the flag, bearing a single red maple leaf.

General

1. It is appropriate for the Canadian Flag to be flown or displayed by individuals and organizations; but at all times the Flag should be treated with dignity and respect and flown or displayed properly.

2. When possible the Flag is flown daily from sunrise to sunset at all federal government buildings, airports, and military bases and establishments within and outside Canada. It is not contrary to etiquette to have the Flag flying at night.

3. The Flag may be displayed flat or flown on a staff. If flat, it may be hung horizontally or vertically. If it hangs vertically against a wall, the Flag should be placed so that the upper part of the leaf is to the left and the stem is to the right as seen by spectators.

4. The Flag may be flown or displayed in a church, auditorium, or other meeting place. When used in the chancel of a church or on a speaker's platform the Flag should be flown to the right of the clergyman or speaker. When used in the body of a church or auditorium the Flag should be flown to the right of the audience or congregation. The Flag should not be used to cover a speaker's table or be draped in front of the platform; nor should it be allowed to touch the floor. If displayed flat against the wall at the back of a platform, the Flag should be above and behind the speaker.

5. When used on the occasion of unveiling a monument, tablet, picture, etc., the Flag should be properly draped and prevented from falling to the ground or floor.

6. In a procession, where several flags are carried, the Canadian Flag should be in the position of honour at the marching right or at the centre front.

The Canadian Flag is on the right of the speaker.

7. The Flag should not be used for commercial advertising purposes. It is quite appropriate to fly it at business establishments or to display it to identify Canadian exhibits at fairs. Its use in such cases, as in all others, should reflect respect for the Flag.

Flown with other Flags

8. No flag, banner or pennant should be flown or displayed above the Canadian Flag.

9. Flags flown together should be approximately the same size and flown from separate staffs at the same height.

10. The Canadian Flag should be given the place of honour when flown or displayed with other flags:
(a) When two or more than three flags are flown together, the Canadian Flag should be on the left as seen by spectators in front of the flags; if a number of countries are represented, the Canadian Flag may be flown at each end of a line of flags.
(b) When three flags are flown together, the Canadian Flag should occupy the central position, with the next ranking flag to the left and third ranking flag to the right, as seen by spectators in front of the flags.
(c) Where more than one flag is flown and it is impossible to hoist or lower them at the same time, the Canadian Flag(s) should be hoisted first and lowered last.

Destruction

11. When a flag becomes worn, noticeably faded or otherwise unfit for service, it should be disposed of privately by burning.

Half-masting

12. The position of the Flag when flying at half-mast will depend on its size, the length of the flagstaff and its location; but as a general rule, the centre of a flag should be exactly half-way down the staff. When hoisted to or lowered from half-mast position, a flag should first be raised to the masthead.

13. (a) Subject to (c) and (e), or special instructions issued under (d), the Flag on the Peace Tower of the Parliament Buildings, Ottawa, is flown at half-mast on the death of the Sovereign or a member of the Royal Family related in the

Carry the Canadian Flag at the marching right or at the centre front.

first degree to the Sovereign (that is to say, husband or wife, son or daughter, father, mother or brother or sister), the Governor General, a former Governor General, a Lieutenant-Governor, a Canadian Privy Councillor, a Senator, or a Member of the House of Commons.

(b) Subject to (c) and (e) or special instructions issued under (d), the Flag on other federal government buildings, airports, and military bases and establishments is flown at half-mast

(i) throughout Canada, on the death of the Sovereign or a member of the Royal Family related in the first degree to the Sovereign, the Governor General, the Prime Minister of Canada, a former Governor General, a former Prime Minister of Canada, or a federal Cabinet Minister;

(ii) within a province, on the death of the Lieutenant-Governor, the Provincial Premier, or another person similarly honoured by that province;

(iii) within his own riding, on the death of the Member of the House of Commons, or the Member of the Provincial Legislature;

(iv) at his place of residence, on the death of a Senator, a Canadian Privy Councillor, or a Mayor.

(c) "Death" for the purposes of (a) and (b) may be taken to include the day of death and up to and including the day of the funeral.

(d) Flags at federal buildings and other locations are also half-masted subject to special instructions on the death of members of the Royal Family other than the Sovereign or those related in the first degree to the Sovereign, a Head of a Foreign State, or some other person whom it is desired to honour.

(e) During periods of half-masting, the Flag is raised to full-mast on all federal buildings, airports and military bases and establishments on statutory holidays, and also on the Peace Tower while a Head of State is visiting Parliament Hill; but this procedure does *not* apply while flags are half-masted for the death of the Sovereign when they are only raised to full-mast for the day on which the accession of the new Monarch is proclaimed.

(f) On Remembrance Day, November 11th, the Flag is flown at half-mast at 11:00 a.m. on the Peace Tower of the Parliament Buildings.

When three flags are flown together.